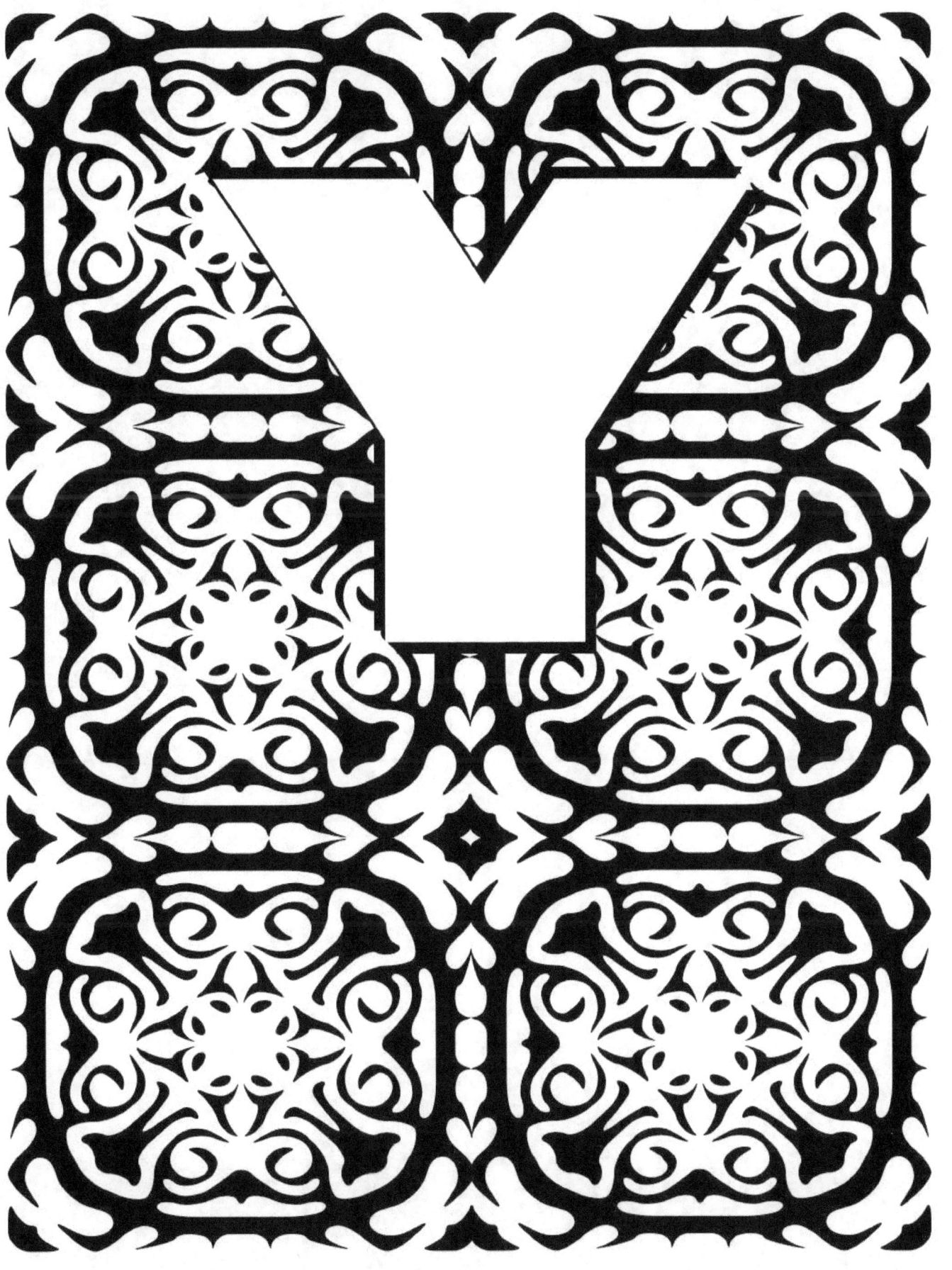

A Is For Angle

B Is For Bless

C Is For Cute

D Is For Do

E Is For Enjoy

F Is For First

G Is For Good

H Is For Heaven

I Is For Idea

J Is For Joy

K Is For Kind

L Is For Life

M Is For Make

N Is For Nice

O Is For Open

P Is For Polite

Q Is For Quiet

R Is For Right

S Is For Super

T Is For Tidy

U Is For Understand

V Is For Value

W Is For Warm

X Is For XXL

Y Is For Youth

Z Is For Zest

HALLOWEEN

www.ingramcontent.com/pod-product-compliance
Lightning Source LLC
LaVergne TN
LVHW060141080526
838202LV00049B/4045